WORKAHOLICS™

Adult **MAD LiBS**®

by Brian D. Clark

PRICE STERN SLOAN

An Imprint of Penguin Random House

PRICE STERN SLOAN
An Imprint of Penguin Random House LLC

Mad Libs format copyright © 2015 by Price Stern Sloan,
an imprint of Penguin Random House LLC. All rights reserved.

Concept created by Roger Price & Leonard Stern.

© 2015 Comedy Partners. All rights reserved. Comedy Central, Workaholics and all related titles,
logos and characters are trademarks of Comedy Partners

Published by Price Stern Sloan, an imprint of Penguin Random House LLC,
345 Hudson Street, New York, New York 10014.
Printed in the USA.

ISBN 978-0-8431-8278-1

1 3 5 7 9 10 8 6 4 2

MAD LIBS® is a game for people who don't like games!
It can be played by one, two, three, four, or forty.

• RIDICULOUSLY SIMPLE DIRECTIONS

In this book, you'll find stories containing blank spaces where words are left out. One player, the READER, selects one of the stories. The READER shouldn't tell anyone what the story is about. Instead, the READER should ask the other players, the WRITERS, to give words to fill in the blank spaces in the story.

• TO PLAY

The READER asks each WRITER in turn to call out words—adjectives or nouns or whatever the spaces call for—and uses them to fill in the blank spaces in the story. The result is your very own MAD LIBS! Then, when the READER reads the completed MAD LIBS to the other players, they will discover they have written a story that is fantastic, screamingly funny, shocking, silly, crazy, or just plain dumb— depending on the words each WRITER called out.

• EXAMPLE (*Before* and *After*)

" _____ !" he said _____
      EXCLAMATION   ADVERB

as he jumped into his convertible _____ and
                                                        NOUN

drove off with his _____ wife.
                              ADJECTIVE

" *Ouch* !" he said *stupidly*
      EXCLAMATION   ADVERB

as he jumped into his convertible *cat* and
                                                        NOUN

drove off with his *brave* wife.
                              ADJECTIVE

In case you have forgotten what adjectives, adverbs, nouns, and verbs are, here is a quick review:

An **ADJECTIVE** describes something or somebody. *Lumpy, soft, ugly, messy,* and *short* are adjectives.

An **ADVERB** tells how something is done. It modifies a verb and usually ends in "ly." *Modestly, stupidly, greedily,* and *carefully* are adverbs.

A **NOUN** is the name of a person, place, or thing. *Sidewalk, umbrella, bridle, bathtub,* and *nose* are nouns.

A **VERB** is an action word. *Run, pitch, jump,* and *swim* are verbs. Put the verbs in past tense if the directions say **PAST TENSE.** *Ran, pitched, jumped,* and *swam* are verbs in the past tense.

When we ask for **A PLACE,** we mean any sort of place: a country or city (*Spain, Cleveland*) or a room (*bathroom, kitchen*).

An **EXCLAMATION** or **SILLY WORD** is any sort of funny sound, gasp, grunt, or outcry, like *Wow!, Ouch!, Whomp!, Ick!,* and *Gadzooks!*

When we ask for specific words, like a **NUMBER,** a **COLOR,** an **ANIMAL,** or a **PART OF THE BODY,** we mean a word that is one of those things, like *seven, blue, horse,* or *head.*

When we ask for a **PLURAL,** it means more than one. For example, *cat* pluralized is *cats.*

MAD LIBS® is fun to play with friends, but you can also play it by yourself! To begin with, DO NOT look at the story on the page below. Fill in the blanks on this page with the words called for. Then, using the words you have selected, fill in the blank spaces in the story. Now you've created your own hilarious MAD LIBS® game!

ADJECTIVE _____

NOUN _____

NOUN _____

SILLY WORD _____

PART OF THE BODY (PLURAL) _____

VERB ENDING IN "ING" _____

VEHICLE _____

ARTICLE OF CLOTHING _____

NUMBER _____

PLURAL NOUN _____

PLURAL NOUN _____

ADJECTIVE _____

SILLY WORD _____

VERB _____

ANIMAL _____

VERB _____

PART OF THE BODY _____

EXCLAMATION _____

Anders, Blake, and Adam are _____ friends, and there's

ADJECTIVE

nothing that can break that _____—even if their boss says

NOUN

they're a bunch of immature _____-husbands living in a broje-

NOUN

et-_____! These three have one another's _____

SILLY WORD   PART OF THE BODY (PLURAL)

whether they're just _____ in the _____, mooching

VERB ENDING IN "ING"   VEHICLE

Anders's clean _____, pounding _____ beers every night,

ARTICLE OF CLOTHING   NUMBER

or bringing loaded _____ to the office. Good _____!

PLURAL NOUN   PLURAL NOUN

But it's when times get _____ that you really need a true

ADJECTIVE

_____ at your side! Like when a drug dealer is out to

SILLY WORD

_____ you for nonpayment, or when you're all hallucinating

VERB

that a giant _____ is trying to _____ your _____

ANIMAL   VERB   PART OF THE BODY

off! _____!

EXCLAMATION

From ADULT MAD LIBS®: Workaholics™ Mad Libs • © 2015 Comedy Partners. All rights reserved.
Published by Price Stern Sloan, an imprint of Penguin Random House LLC, 345 Hudson Street, New York, New York 10014.

Adult MAD LiBS

WORDS OF WISDOM FROM BLAKE

The world's greatest _office_ game

MAD LIBS® is fun to play with friends, but you can also play it by yourself! To begin with, DO NOT look at the story on the page below. Fill in the blanks on this page with the words called for. Then, using the words you have selected, fill in the blank spaces in the story. Now you've created your own hilarious MAD LIBS® game!

PLURAL NOUN _____

PART OF THE BODY _____

NOUN _____

NOUN _____

PERSON IN ROOM _____

COLOR _____

NOUN _____

SILLY WORD _____

SILLY WORD _____

ADJECTIVE _____

VERB _____

OCCUPATION _____

A PLACE _____

NOUN _____

ADJECTIVE _____

ADVERB _____

PLURAL NOUN _____

Here are some _____ of wisdom that are sure to blow your
PLURAL NOUN

_____. First, when trying to buy _____ from a
PART OF THE BODY   NOUN

_____ dealer you don't trust, like _____, change how you
NOUN   PERSON IN ROOM

pronounce the important words to avoid getting busted by the men

in _____. For example, instead of saying you want to smoke
COLOR

some "_____," say _____. Instead of saying "bowl,"
NOUN   SILLY WORD

say _____. Also, if you need an excuse to go home sick from
SILLY WORD

work even though you are feeling totally _____, just make
ADJECTIVE

yourself _____ your lunch! Then your _____ will think
VERB   OCCUPATION

you're sick and send you to (the) _____ early. It's basically a
A PLACE

get-out-of-_____-free pass! Oh, and the most _____
NOUN   ADJECTIVE

rule ever—never get into a fight when your bone is _____
ADVERB

torqued. Everyone knows that _____ cannot collide when erect.
PLURAL NOUN

MAD LIBS® is fun to play with friends, but you can also play it by yourself! To begin with, DO NOT look at the story on the page below. Fill in the blanks on this page with the words called for. Then, using the words you have selected, fill in the blank spaces in the story. Now you've created your own hilarious MAD LIBS® game!

PLURAL NOUN _____

ADJECTIVE _____

VERB _____

ADJECTIVE _____

PART OF THE BODY _____

VERB ENDING IN "ING" _____

ADJECTIVE _____

NOUN _____

PART OF THE BODY _____

VERB _____

NOUN _____

NOUN _____

PLURAL NOUN _____

ARTICLE OF CLOTHING _____

PLURAL NOUN _____

VERB ENDING IN "ING" _____

COLOR _____

ADJECTIVE _____

It takes a lot of imagination to come up with ingenious _____
                                                      PLURAL NOUN

to the _____ problems Adam, Blake, and Ders _____
        ADJECTIVE   VERB

on a daily basis. Not to mention some _____ old-fashioned
                                        ADJECTIVE

_____ grease! For example, if you're trying to hide that
PART OF THE BODY

you're _____ alcohol in the office, consider attaching
       VERB ENDING IN "ING"

a/an _____ _____ of vodka to your telephone
     ADJECTIVE   NOUN

_____-set, so you can drink while you _____ on the
PART OF THE BODY   VERB

phone. If your sex _____ is dirty, wash it with the rest of the
                    NOUN

dishes in the office _____-washer. And if you're really into
                      NOUN

enjoying the great _____ but are on a/an _____-string
                    PLURAL NOUN   ARTICLE OF CLOTHING

budget, you can set up some folding _____ on your roof to
                                     PLURAL NOUN

enjoy _____ a beautiful _____ sunset with your
       VERB ENDING IN "ING"   COLOR

_____ friends.
ADJECTIVE

From ADULT MAD LIBS®: Workaholics™ Mad Libs • © 2015 Comedy Partners. All rights reserved.
Published by Price Stern Sloan, an imprint of Penguin Random House LLC, 345 Hudson Street, New York, New York 10014.

Adult MAD LiBS®

ANDERS'S RAP

The world's greatest *office* game

MAD LIBS® is fun to play with friends, but you can also play it by yourself! To begin with, DO NOT look at the story on the page below. Fill in the blanks on this page with the words called for. Then, using the words you have selected, fill in the blank spaces in the story. Now you've created your own hilarious MAD LIBS® game!

EXCLAMATION _____

PERSON IN ROOM _____

NOUN _____

ANIMAL _____

ADJECTIVE _____

PART OF THE BODY (PLURAL) _____

NOUN _____

ARTICLE OF CLOTHING (PLURAL) _____

OCCUPATION _____

VERB _____

PLURAL NOUN _____

TYPE OF LIQUID _____

SILLY WORD _____

NOUN _____

ADJECTIVE _____

PERSON IN ROOM _____

_____! My name is MC _____ and I'm the king of
EXCLAMATION   PERSON IN ROOM

_____!
NOUN

There isn't a girl's _____ that my _____ rhymes
ANIMAL   ADJECTIVE

can't tap!

You know my swimmer's _____ are something to fear.
PART OF THE BODY (PLURAL)

Cuz when I flex them like a/an _____ it makes the ladies'
NOUN

_____ disappear.
ARTICLE OF CLOTHING (PLURAL)

And when I roll up to the club, the _____ doesn't even
OCCUPATION

_____ my money!
VERB

He knows I attract hot _____ like bees to _____!
PLURAL NOUN   TYPE OF LIQUID

So watch them lose their _____ when I hit the dance
SILLY WORD

_____!
NOUN

Cuz my moves make those _____ bitches scream for more!
ADJECTIVE

MC _____, out! Yo!
PERSON IN ROOM

MAD LIBS® is fun to play with friends, but you can also play it by yourself! To begin with, DO NOT look at the story on the page below. Fill in the blanks on this page with the words called for. Then, using the words you have selected, fill in the blank spaces in the story. Now you've created your own hilarious MAD LIBS® game!

NOUN _____

NOUN _____

VERB ENDING IN "ING" _____

ARTICLE OF CLOTHING _____

PART OF THE BODY _____

VERB _____

ADJECTIVE _____

TYPE OF LIQUID _____

ADJECTIVE _____

ADVERB _____

NOUN _____

SAME NOUN _____

NOUN _____

ADJECTIVE _____

ADVERB _____

PLURAL NOUN _____

TelAmeri-_____ has strict rules of _____ in place to
NOUN   NOUN

keep all employees _____ efficiently.
VERB ENDING IN "ING"

- Do wear a shirt and _____ to work. Underwear is also
ARTICLE OF CLOTHING

  required and not to be worn on your _____.
PART OF THE BODY

- Do not _____ off in the restroom, no matter how long
VERB

  you've had a raging _____-on.
ADJECTIVE

- Drinking beer, _____, or any other _____
TYPE OF LIQUID   ADJECTIVE

  beverages is _____ prohibited.
ADVERB

- No one is allowed in my _____. Any employee found
NOUN

  in my _____, sitting at my _____, or looking
SAME NOUN   NOUN

  through my _____ emails will be _____
ADJECTIVE   ADVERB

  terminated.

- Foul language is not permitted under any _____!
PLURAL NOUN

The world's greatest *office* game

MAD LIBS® is fun to play with friends, but you can also play it by yourself! To begin with, DO NOT look at the story on the page below. Fill in the blanks on this page with the words called for. Then, using the words you have selected, fill in the blank spaces in the story. Now you've created your own hilarious MAD LIBS® game!

NOUN _____

VERB (PAST TENSE) _____

NUMBER _____

ADJECTIVE _____

PLURAL NOUN _____

NOUN _____

NOUN _____

PART OF THE BODY _____

PART OF THE BODY (PLURAL) _____

ANIMAL _____

ADJECTIVE _____

PART OF THE BODY _____

ADJECTIVE _____

VERB _____

PLURAL NOUN _____

Adult MAD LiBS®
WE KNOW CHICKS

The world's greatest _office_ game

Adam, Ders, and Blake know _____—maybe because they've
                                    NOUN

cumulatively _____ no less than _____ women. Anders
                VERB (PAST TENSE)   NUMBER

is the _____-hitter of the group. He's at least scored in the
            ADJECTIVE

double-_____ and managed to be suave in front of a Swedish
          PLURAL NOUN

_____ pal while at a memorial service for a dead _____.
    NOUN   NOUN

Adam is the master of _____ thrusts and loves to show off
                          PART OF THE BODY

his moves by groaning and kicking his _____ back like
                                          PART OF THE BODY (PLURAL)

a/an _____! As for Blake, well, it's pretty clear Blake is a/an
          ANIMAL

_____ virgin. But with that long, curly _____ and his
    ADJECTIVE   PART OF THE BODY

_____ smile, it's only a matter time before he gets someone to
    ADJECTIVE

_____ in between the _____ with him.
    VERB   PLURAL NOUN

Adult MAD LiBS®

WELCOME TO THE MUSCLE FACTORY

The world's greatest _office_ game

MAD LIBS® is fun to play with friends, but you can also play it by yourself! To begin with, DO NOT look at the story on the page below. Fill in the blanks on this page with the words called for. Then, using the words you have selected, fill in the blank spaces in the story. Now you've created your own hilarious MAD LIBS® game!

PERSON IN ROOM (MALE) _____

ADJECTIVE _____

NOUN _____

COLOR _____

VERB ENDING IN "ING" _____

OCCUPATION _____

NOUN _____

ADJECTIVE _____

NOUN _____

SILLY WORD _____

PART OF THE BODY (PLURAL) _____

NOUN _____

EXCLAMATION _____

ADJECTIVE _____

_____ is awesome! In fact, everything about him is totally
PERSON IN ROOM (MALE)

_____. He usually demonstrates his awesome, masculine
ADJECTIVE

_____ by getting all slicked up in _____ oil for
NOUN   COLOR

body-_____ competitions or by deciding to be a male
VERB ENDING IN "ING"

_____, like the kind they have on the cover of _____
OCCUPATION   NOUN

Magazine. He's so _____, he even created his own workout
ADJECTIVE

_____ called De-_____ Camp, which was going really
NOUN   SILLY WORD

well until he dislocated both of his _____ by trying to lift a
PART OF THE BODY (PLURAL)

giant _____. _____! That probably hurt, but not that
NOUN   EXCLAMATION

bad since he's so _____.
ADJECTIVE

From ADULT MAD LIBS®: Workaholics™ Mad Libs • © 2015 Comedy Partners. All rights reserved.
Published by Price Stern Sloan, an imprint of Penguin Random House LLC, 345 Hudson Street, New York, New York 10014.

MAD LIBS® is fun to play with friends, but you can also play it by yourself! To begin with, DO NOT look at the story on the page below. Fill in the blanks on this page with the words called for. Then, using the words you have selected, fill in the blank spaces in the story. Now you've created your own hilarious MAD LIBS® game!

ADJECTIVE _____

NOUN _____

SILLY WORD _____

PART OF THE BODY _____

ANIMAL (PLURAL) _____

PLURAL NOUN _____

PERSON IN ROOM _____

SAME PERSON IN ROOM _____

PART OF THE BODY _____

CELEBRITY (MALE) _____

EXCLAMATION _____

VERB ENDING IN "ING" _____

NOUN _____

VERB _____

ADJECTIVE _____

VERB (PAST TENSE) _____

ADJECTIVE _____

ANIMAL _____

Anders is always eager to impress his father and uphold the honor of

his _____ heritage. That's why he calls his _____ "Sir,"
      ADJECTIVE   NOUN

and why he cooks Norwegian foods like kjott-_____-er, cod
                                            SILLY WORD

_____, and soup that has salty _____ floating in it. It's
PART OF THE BODY   ANIMAL (PLURAL)

also why he was ashamed to tell his dad that he's best _____
                                                        PLURAL NOUN

with _____ and Blake. And good thing, too, because when
     PERSON IN ROOM

they met Mr. Holmvik, _____ asked if Ders's dad called his
                       SAME PERSON IN ROOM

_____ " _____'s Hammer." _____! Good thing
PART OF THE BODY   CELEBRITY (MALE)   EXCLAMATION

Anders covered by _____ into the _____ across the
                  VERB ENDING IN "ING"   NOUN

street that was for sale and pretended to _____ there, so his dad
                                           VERB

would think he's _____ rich. That is, until his father revealed
                 ADJECTIVE

that he _____ his job and the two shared a/an _____
        VERB (PAST TENSE)   ADJECTIVE

hug over some very wet _____ jerky.
                       ANIMAL

From ADULT MAD LIBS®: Workaholics™ Mad Libs • © 2015 Comedy Partners. All rights reserved.
Published by Price Stern Sloan, an imprint of Penguin Random House LLC, 345 Hudson Street, New York, New York 10014.

MAD LIBS® is fun to play with friends, but you can also play it by yourself! To begin with, DO NOT look at the story on the page below. Fill in the blanks on this page with the words called for. Then, using the words you have selected, fill in the blank spaces in the story. Now you've created your own hilarious MAD LIBS® game!

ADJECTIVE _____

OCCUPATION (PLURAL) _____

NUMBER _____

PLURAL NOUN _____

VERB _____

PLURAL NOUN _____

TYPE OF LIQUID _____

NOUN _____

ANIMAL _____

NOUN _____

VERB (PAST TENSE) _____

PLURAL NOUN _____

ADVERB _____

NOUN _____

PLURAL NOUN _____

NOUN _____

NOUN _____

Adam, Anders, and Blake are by far the most _____
                                                    ADJECTIVE
_____ in all of TelAmeriCorp's _____ _____.
OCCUPATION (PLURAL)   NUMBER   PLURAL NOUN
Their sales continually fail to meet or _____ expectations,
                                              VERB
mostly because they're always making prank calls to senior

_____ or deciding whether or not to use one another's
PLURAL NOUN

_____ to pass random _____ tests. Their attempts
TYPE OF LIQUID   NOUN

to have a/an _____ fry in the office and to join the office
                 ANIMAL

_____-ball team back-_____ and nearly reduced office
NOUN   VERB (PAST TENSE)

morale to _____. They _____ torture their coworkers
          PLURAL NOUN   ADVERB

by putting boiling _____ in their coffee _____ or by
                        NOUN   PLURAL NOUN

constantly making them pick up a poop _____. In short, their
                                            NOUN

performance really needs _____!
                              NOUN

MAD LIBS® is fun to play with friends, but you can also play it by yourself! To begin with, DO NOT look at the story on the page below. Fill in the blanks on this page with the words called for. Then, using the words you have selected, fill in the blank spaces in the story. Now you've created your own hilarious MAD LIBS® game!

NOUN _____

PLURAL NOUN _____

NUMBER _____

VEHICLE _____

ADVERB _____

ADJECTIVE _____

PART OF THE BODY (PLURAL) _____

ADJECTIVE _____

ADJECTIVE _____

NOUN _____

SILLY WORD _____

PERSON IN ROOM (MALE) _____

NOUN _____

PART OF THE BODY _____

VERB _____

NOUN _____

Karl knows how to make a living while giving back to society. And

not just by being a/an _____ dealer! People think that just
NOUN

because you sell illegal _____ to _____-year-old kids
PLURAL NOUN   _NUMBER_

and drive a/an _____, that you don't have a heart. But they're
VEHICLE

_____ wrong! Karl is one of the most _____ guys
ADVERB   _ADJECTIVE_

you'll ever lay _____ on. Karl gives _____ tourists
PART OF THE BODY (PLURAL)   _ADJECTIVE_

Hollywood tours in a/an _____ tub, gives massages to the
ADJECTIVE

_____-less, and even donated his one-eyed _____
NOUN   _SILLY WORD_

to _____ just because he felt bad that Blake's _____
PERSON IN ROOM (MALE)   _NOUN_

was so small. But then Blake changed his _____ and made
PART OF THE BODY

the doctor _____ his wiener back on. One good _____
VERB   _NOUN_

deserves another!

MAD LIBS® is fun to play with friends, but you can also play it by yourself! To begin with, DO NOT look at the story on the page below. Fill in the blanks on this page with the words called for. Then, using the words you have selected, fill in the blank spaces in the story. Now you've created your own hilarious MAD LIBS® game!

PERSON IN ROOM (MALE) _____

ADJECTIVE _____

OCCUPATION (PLURAL) _____

NOUN _____

NOUN _____

VERB ENDING IN "ING" _____

ADJECTIVE _____

ANIMAL _____

VERB ENDING IN "ING" _____

PERSON IN ROOM (FEMALE) _____

NOUN _____

NOUN _____

ADJECTIVE _____

PART OF THE BODY _____

PERSON IN ROOM (MALE) _____

Montez and Waymond do not get along with Blake, Anders,

and _____, and it's not only because, as _____
    PERSON IN ROOM (MALE)   ADJECTIVE

_____, they all had to compete to win a sweet-ass
OCCUPATION (PLURAL)

_____ with a/an _____ built in the door. It's because the guys
   NOUN   NOUN

are always _____ with them! Montez is always angry because
         VERB ENDING IN "ING"

he thinks they are _____ bitches who stole his _____
        ADJECTIVE   ANIMAL

cream cheese, and because they get grossed out by his stories about

_____ his wife, _____, on a plastic _____ while
VERB ENDING IN "ING"   PERSON IN ROOM (FEMALE)   NOUN

slathered in _____ oil. Though he doesn't say much, Waymond
           NOUN

shows his _____ feelings by giving the middle _____
       ADJECTIVE   PART OF THE BODY

to people in the office he hates, especially _____.
                                       PERSON IN ROOM (MALE)

MAD LIBS® is fun to play with friends, but you can also play it by yourself! To begin with, DO NOT look at the story on the page below. Fill in the blanks on this page with the words called for. Then, using the words you have selected, fill in the blank spaces in the story. Now you've created your own hilarious MAD LIBS® game!

NOUN _____

ADJECTIVE _____

ADVERB _____

VERB _____

ADJECTIVE _____

PLURAL NOUN _____

ANIMAL _____

VERB _____

SILLY WORD _____

NUMBER _____

ANIMAL _____

TYPE OF LIQUID _____

VERB _____

ARTICLE OF CLOTHING (PLURAL) _____

ADJECTIVE _____

NOUN _____

ADJECTIVE _____

SILLY WORD _____

Adult MAD LiBS® PARTY CRUSHERS

The world's greatest _office_ game

It's always _____ time when you share a house with your
                 NOUN

_____ buds! But if you really want your party to be
     ADJECTIVE

_____ epic, you'll need to do more than just _____ up the
   ADVERB   VERB

stereo, buy some _____-shelf liquor, and invite over a few hot
                    ADJECTIVE

_____ in _____-boy hats. You need to _____
 PLURAL NOUN   ANIMAL   VERB

all in! To really jump-start any party, allow your guests to take a

picture with a dead Rancho Cupa-_____-braj! If that doesn't
                                  SILLY WORD

work, float a/an _____-_____-power hovercraft in
                  NUMBER   ANIMAL

the pool or build a homemade _____-slide! But remember
                               TYPE OF LIQUID

to _____ your audience. Your guests may not to want strip
     VERB

off their _____ to taste your _____ Jungle Juice,
        ARTICLE OF CLOTHING (PLURAL)   ADJECTIVE

especially if they were expecting a World of _____ Murder
                                               NOUN

Mystery Party. Either way, it's time to party _____-core. This
                                                 ADJECTIVE

_____ is going to be insane!
 SILLY WORD

MAD LIBS® is fun to play with friends, but you can also play it by yourself! To begin with, DO NOT look at the story on the page below. Fill in the blanks on this page with the words called for. Then, using the words you have selected, fill in the blank spaces in the story. Now you've created your own hilarious MAD LIBS® game!

ADJECTIVE _____

SILLY WORD _____

VERB _____

OCCUPATION _____

PERSON IN ROOM _____

PART OF THE BODY _____

ADJECTIVE _____

VERB _____

PLURAL NOUN _____

PART OF THE BODY _____

NOUN _____

ADJECTIVE _____

TYPE OF LIQUID _____

VEHICLE _____

ADVERB _____

VERB _____

Everyone needs a/an _____-ass ride. Their ride, which the boys
                        ADJECTIVE

call the _____, is Blake, Anders, and Adam's vehicle of choice.
            SILLY WORD

They use it to make a quick _____- away from the neighborhood
                                VERB

security _____ and to roll up gangsta-style on Waymond
            OCCUPATION

and _____ to shoot them in the _____ with darts. In
        PERSON IN ROOM   PART OF THE BODY

_____ emergencies, the car can also be used to _____
   ADJECTIVE   VERB

in during a stroke break, as long as you hang _____ between
                                                 PLURAL NOUN

the seats so no one's _____ gets in your crank zone. This car
                        PART OF THE BODY

has a/an _____ big enough to hold Alice's brother and a hood
            NOUN

_____ enough to land on after jumping from a/an _____
   ADJECTIVE   TYPE OF LIQUID

truck during a beer heist. And even though this "classic" _____
                                                             VEHICLE

is _____ trashed, with regularly scheduled maintenance this
      ADVERB

car will _____ forever!
            VERB

MAD LIBS® is fun to play with friends, but you can also play it by yourself! To begin with, DO NOT look at the story on the page below. Fill in the blanks on this page with the words called for. Then, using the words you have selected, fill in the blank spaces in the story. Now you've created your own hilarious MAD LIBS® game!

ADJECTIVE _____

ANIMAL (PLURAL) _____

NOUN _____

ADJECTIVE _____

PART OF THE BODY _____

NOUN _____

ADVERB _____

PERSON IN ROOM (MALE) _____

ANIMAL _____

NOUN _____

VERB _____

ADJECTIVE _____

NOUN _____

VERB _____

NOUN _____

Adult MAD LiBS®

JILLIAN FROM THE INSIDE

The world's greatest *office* game

Alice's _____ assistant, Jillian, knows her way around the office
ADJECTIVE

better than her many kitty-_____ know their way around the
ANIMAL (PLURAL)

_____ box. Working for Alice is usually as _____ as pie,
NOUN   ADJECTIVE

if Jillian keeps her _____ shut, gets whatever the _____
PART OF THE BODY   NOUN

Alice wants on her bagel, and hides that she is _____ in love with
ADVERB

her coworker _____. Jillian wants him to hook into her like a
PERSON IN ROOM (MALE)

rabid dire _____ banging a lioness. But there's more to Jillian
ANIMAL

than a strong _____ ethic and her deep need to _____
NOUN   VERB

really hard. Ultimately she's looking for a true _____ companion
ADJECTIVE

who she can spend every day of her _____ with until they
NOUN

_____ on the exact same day. Exact same _____.
VERB   NOUN

The world's greatest _office_ game

MAD LIBS® is fun to play with friends, but you can also play it by yourself! To begin with, DO NOT look at the story on the page below. Fill in the blanks on this page with the words called for. Then, using the words you have selected, fill in the blank spaces in the story. Now you've created your own hilarious MAD LIBS® game!

ADJECTIVE _____

VERB ENDING IN "ING" _____

PLURAL NOUN _____

PART OF THE BODY _____

ADJECTIVE _____

VERB _____

NOUN _____

ARTICLE OF CLOTHING _____

COLOR _____

NOUN _____

ADVERB _____

NUMBER _____

TYPE OF FOOD _____

PLURAL NOUN _____

NOUN _____

NOUN _____

ARTICLE OF CLOTHING _____

VERB (PAST TENSE) _____

Adult MAD LiBS® THE DAY AFTER

The world's greatest *office* game

Partying is fun, but if you're not careful, the next morning can be

_____. Consider yourself lucky if you escape a night of binge
  ADJECTIVE

_____ with just a few bumps and _____ on your
  VERB ENDING IN "ING"   PLURAL NOUN

_____ and a/an _____ _____-over; or if you
  PART OF THE BODY   ADJECTIVE   VERB

wake up in the _____ of your car with your _____ on
                  NOUN   ARTICLE OF CLOTHING

the outside of your pants and your hair dyed _____! But, if
                                                COLOR

you crashed your neighbor's _____ pride party, _____
                              NOUN   ADVERB

smashed their _____-tiered _____, and woke up
                NUMBER   TYPE OF FOOD

nearly naked in bed with your two best _____, it might be
                                          PLURAL NOUN

time to seek professional _____. If so, enroll yourself in a/an
                            NOUN

_____-abuse course where you can use _____ puppets
  NOUN   ARTICLE OF CLOTHING

to express your true feelings. Problem _____!
                                         VERB (PAST TENSE)

From ADULT MAD LIBS®: Workaholics™ Mad Libs • © 2015 Comedy Partners. All rights reserved.
Published by Price Stern Sloan, an imprint of Penguin Random House LLC, 345 Hudson Street, New York, New York 10014.

MAD LIBS® is fun to play with friends, but you can also play it by yourself! To begin with, DO NOT look at the story on the page below. Fill in the blanks on this page with the words called for. Then, using the words you have selected, fill in the blank spaces in the story. Now you've created your own hilarious MAD LIBS® game!

A PLACE _____

NUMBER _____

ADJECTIVE _____

NOUN _____

TYPE OF LIQUID _____

PLURAL NOUN _____

ADJECTIVE _____

LETTER OF THE ALPHABET _____

ANIMAL _____

COLOR _____

ARTICLE OF CLOTHING _____

PLURAL NOUN _____

NOUN _____

NOUN _____

NOUN _____

Celebrating Half Christmas in your own _____ is as
A PLACE

easy as one, two, _____. To bring _____ tidings
NUMBER ADJECTIVE

and spread the holiday _____, all you need is a full keg of
NOUN

_____, plenty of blinking _____, and of course,
TYPE OF LIQUID PLURAL NOUN

a/an _____ attitude. And remember, nothing says holiday like
ADJECTIVE

the smell of a bar-_____-cued Christmas _____! To
LETTER OF THE ALPHABET ANIMAL

really set the mood you can even put on a red and _____ Santa
COLOR

_____ and go caroling at your neighbor's house. Everyone
ARTICLE OF CLOTHING

loves to deck the _____ with boughs of _____ in July!
PLURAL NOUN NOUN

Who knows, you might even look out the window and see some Half

Christmas _____-flakes as they fall to the ground! Wouldn't
NOUN

that be a Half _____ miracle?
NOUN

The world's greatest _office_ game

MAD LIBS® is fun to play with friends, but you can also play it by yourself! To begin with, DO NOT look at the story on the page below. Fill in the blanks on this page with the words called for. Then, using the words you have selected, fill in the blank spaces in the story. Now you've created your own hilarious MAD LIBS® game!

NOUN _____

PART OF THE BODY _____

NOUN _____

ADJECTIVE _____

VERB _____

NOUN _____

NOUN _____

EXCLAMATION _____

PART OF THE BODY _____

OCCUPATION _____

SILLY WORD _____

CELEBRITY _____

NOUN _____

ADJECTIVE _____

ADJECTIVE _____

NOUN _____

Adult MAD LiBS

MONTEZ WALKER'S GUIDE TO LOVEMAKING

The world's greatest _office_ game

Montez knows how to please a/an _____ in the bedroom!

NOUN

His wife, the most bangin'-_____ woman in the whole

PART OF THE BODY

_____, is an example. Even after ten _____ years

NOUN   ADJECTIVE

of marriage, she still wants to _____ the _____ out

VERB   NOUN

of him morning, noon, and _____! _____! That's

NOUN   EXCLAMATION

because he knows how to play his wife's _____ like he's a/an

PART OF THE BODY

_____ and she's his violin. Once she's all fired up, he'll scream,

OCCUPATION

"_____," just like _____ of the jungle! Then he lays

SILLY WORD   CELEBRITY

out the _____, gets out that good-ass _____ oil, and

NOUN   ADJECTIVE

gets in it! He always uses a/an _____ touch! After all, she's a

ADJECTIVE

classy _____, especially since Montez got her all pregnatized!

NOUN

From ADULT MAD LIBS®: Workaholics™ Mad Libs • © 2015 Comedy Partners. All rights reserved.
Published by Price Stern Sloan, an imprint of Penguin Random House LLC, 345 Hudson Street, New York, New York 10014.

Adult MAD LiBS®

OFFICE PAYBACKS

The world's greatest *office* game

MAD LIBS® is fun to play with friends, but you can also play it by yourself! To begin with, DO NOT look at the story on the page below. Fill in the blanks on this page with the words called for. Then, using the words you have selected, fill in the blank spaces in the story. Now you've created your own hilarious MAD LIBS® game!

NOUN _____

OCCUPATION (PLURAL) _____

ADJECTIVE _____

A PLACE _____

PART OF THE BODY (PLURAL) _____

NOUN _____

VERB ENDING IN "ING" _____

TYPE OF FOOD _____

PLURAL NOUN _____

ADJECTIVE _____

NOUN _____

PART OF THE BODY _____

ADJECTIVE _____

OCCUPATION _____

NOUN _____

ADVERB _____

NUMBER _____

NOUN _____

Whether you're out for a good, hearty _____ at the expense of

NOUN

your co-_____ or you're seeking some _____-core

OCCUPATION (PLURAL)   ADJECTIVE

revenge, pranks are a great way to get back at anyone in (the)

_____. You can place fake _____ on the floor of

A PLACE   PART OF THE BODY (PLURAL)

the _____-room stall so people think you're _____, or

NOUN   VERB ENDING IN "ING"

you can prank a sleeping coworker by covering them in _____

TYPE OF FOOD

and other office _____ (just make sure they're sleeping and

PLURAL NOUN

not _____ first). If you want to be original, you could put a/an

ADJECTIVE

_____ lock around your coworker's _____ right before he

NOUN   PART OF THE BODY

goes into a/an _____ meeting with his _____. But if

ADJECTIVE   OCCUPATION

you really just need to blow off some _____, prank your boss

NOUN

by getting _____ drunk and then leaving her _____

ADVERB   NUMBER

thousand prank voicemails! Paybacks are a/an _____.

NOUN

From ADULT MAD LIBS®: Workaholics™ Mad Libs • © 2015 Comedy Partners. All rights reserved.
Published by Price Stern Sloan, an imprint of Penguin Random House LLC, 345 Hudson Street, New York, New York 10014.

Adult MAD LiBS®

ALICE'S "WHY MY JOB SUCKS" LIST

The world's greatest _office_ game

MAD LIBS® is fun to play with friends, but you can also play it by yourself! To begin with, DO NOT look at the story on the page below. Fill in the blanks on this page with the words called for. Then, using the words you have selected, fill in the blank spaces in the story. Now you've created your own hilarious MAD LIBS® game!

ADJECTIVE _____

PART OF THE BODY _____

VERB ENDING IN "ING" _____

OCCUPATION _____

NOUN _____

ADVERB _____

NOUN _____

A PLACE _____

ADJECTIVE _____

PLURAL NOUN _____

VERB _____

NOUN _____

VERB (PAST TENSE) _____

NUMBER _____

TYPE OF FOOD _____

VERB ENDING IN "ING" _____

EXCLAMATION _____

My employees are all a bunch of _____ _____-holes
                                ADJECTIVE   PART OF THE BODY

who want to get paid for _____ around all day.
                           VERB ENDING IN "ING"

- My administrative _____, Jillian, has a brain the size of
                     OCCUPATION

  a/an _____ and is always lurking _____ around
         NOUN   ADVERB

  every _____.
          NOUN

- My bosses at the corporate _____ demand _____
                       A PLACE   ADJECTIVE

  profit margins, even if it means making sales calls to _____
                                                 PLURAL NOUN

  on the do-not-_____ list.
             VERB

- My personal _____ is a disaster, and I never get
                 NOUN

  _____ because I have to work, like, _____ hours
    VERB (PAST TENSE)   NUMBER

  a day.

- The refrigerator in the break room smells like it's got three-month-

  old _____ _____ inside of it. _____!
     TYPE OF FOOD   VERB ENDING IN "ING"   EXCLAMATION

MAD LIBS® is fun to play with friends, but you can also play it by yourself! To begin with, DO NOT look at the story on the page below. Fill in the blanks on this page with the words called for. Then, using the words you have selected, fill in the blank spaces in the story. Now you've created your own hilarious MAD LIBS® game!

VERB _____

NOUN _____

VERB ENDING IN "ING" _____

OCCUPATION (PLURAL) _____

ADJECTIVE _____

NOUN _____

PLURAL NOUN _____

ADJECTIVE _____

NOUN _____

TYPE OF FOOD _____

ANIMAL _____

VERB ENDING IN "ING" _____

NOUN _____

NOUN _____

VERB _____

OCCUPATION _____

STRETCH YOUR MIND

The world's greatest _office_ game

If you want to _____ your mind, you're going to have to think
_{VERB}

outside the _____. For example, if you love _____
_{NOUN} _{VERB ENDING IN "ING"}

the show *American* _____, but are too _____ to get
_{OCCUPATION (PLURAL)} _{ADJECTIVE}

on TV, then re-create the show in your own front _____
_{NOUN}

using some bed _____, _____ tape, and one of
_{PLURAL NOUN} _{ADJECTIVE}

those machines that shoots _____ balls. If you want to own
_{NOUN}

a beef _____ business but don't know how to make jerky,
_{TYPE OF FOOD}

you should probably drag a dead _____ into your bedroom
_{ANIMAL}

and start _____ on it. And if you really want to stretch your
_{VERB ENDING IN "ING"}

_____, try solving a tough problem like creating an *American*
_{NOUN}

_____ that is un-_____-able! Necessity is truly the
_{NOUN} _{VERB}

_____ of invention!
_{OCCUPATION}

Adult MAD LiBS®

MAKING MEMORIES AND THEN DESTROYING THEM

The world's greatest *office* game

MAD LIBS® is fun to play with friends, but you can also play it by yourself! To begin with, DO NOT look at the story on the page below. Fill in the blanks on this page with the words called for. Then, using the words you have selected, fill in the blank spaces in the story. Now you've created your own hilarious MAD LIBS® game!

PLURAL NOUN _____

ADVERB _____

NOUN _____

VERB (PAST TENSE) _____

NOUN _____

OCCUPATION (PLURAL) _____

ADJECTIVE _____

VERB _____

PLURAL NOUN _____

NOUN _____

VEHICLE _____

VERB ENDING IN "ING" _____

VERB _____

ADVERB _____

Adult MAD LiBS®

MAKING MEMORIES AND THEN DESTROYING THEM

The world's greatest *office* game

Anders, Blake, and Adam have made some awesome _____

PLURAL NOUN

together, usually while they're _____ schmacked. They've

ADVERB

driven stolen _____-carts, gotten _____ upside down

NOUN   VERB (PAST TENSE)

in a porta-_____, and been chased by meth _____ who

NOUN   OCCUPATION (PLURAL)

resembled _____ zombies. And that doesn't even include all the

ADJECTIVE

fun they've had trying to _____ goth _____, tripping

VERB   PLURAL NOUN

on _____ while at the office, outwitting tow-_____

NOUN   VEHICLE

drivers, and _____ drunk to avoid a hangover. In the end, they

VERB ENDING IN "ING"

always _____ each other, so it's _____ worth it.

VERB   ADVERB

Download Mad Libs today!

Join the millions of Mad Libs fans creating wacky and wonderful stories on our apps!